Christmas in the Big House,
Christmas in the Quarters

Christmas in the Big House, Christmas in the Quarters

BY PATRICIA C. MCKISSACK AND
FREDRICK L. MCKISSACK

illustrated by John Thompson

SCHOLASTIC INC.
New York Toronto London Auckland Sydney
Mexico City New Delhi Hong Kong

ISBN 0-439-14542-2

Text copyright © 1994 by Patricia C. McKissack
and Fredrick McKissack.

Illustrations copyright © 1994 by John Thompson.

All rights reserved. Published by Scholastic Inc.

SCHOLASTIC and associated logos are trademarks and/or registered
trademarks of Scholastic Inc.

12 11 10 9 8 7 6 5 4 3 2 1   9/9 0 1 2 3 4/0

Printed in the U.S.A.   14

First Scholastic printing, November 1999

The paintings in this book were done in
acrylic on strathmore five-ply kid-finish bristol board.

The red initial capital letters in this book are Tuscan Italian,
an ornamental typeface introduced in 1859.

Designed by Claire B. Counihan

REMEMBERING OUR MANY CHRISTMASES
AT 5900 PERSHING WITH ROBERT,
JOHN, AND FRED, JR.
—P. & F. M.

TO MY WIFE,
DARREN.
—J. T.

CONTENTS

ACKNOWLEDGMENTS

Christmas in the Big House, *Christmas in the Quarters* is set in Virginia, specifically along the James River where the magnificent Tidewater Plantations still stand.

I want to thank Rick Patterson, site administrator at Sully Plantation in Chantilly; Dot Boulware, owner of Edgewood Plantation in Charles City; Adam Scher, curator of Point of Honor Plantation; Melissa G. York, events manager at Oaklands Plantation; and Charles Carter III, owner of Shirley Plantation for their generous help. Without exception they shared family history, supplied information, verified information, and offered suggestions.

Claudia Dunavant of the Giles County Historical Society in Tennessee also has been a great resource person. Her knowledge of and appreciation for Victorian architecture and antebellum customs can only be matched by her hospitality. We will always remember our afternoon of house touring.

Our friend and editor Ann Reit was a constant source of support and encouragement. The input of these people made it possible for us to reconstruct a Virginia plantation circa Christmas 1859, both accurately and honestly. Thank you all.

Patricia and Fredrick McKissack
St. Louis, Missouri

I would like to thank the following people and organizations for their invaluable assistance in producing the illustrations for this book: the Shirley Plantation, the Berkley Plantation, the Evelynton Plantation, the Carter's Grove slave quarters, the Grace Episcopal Church, the Martha Institute, the Cornwall Bridge Pottery, the Phoenix Ensemble, Charmaine Tarawally, Dave Robinson, Tony Wilkes, Khayree Wilkes, Marsha Trice, Saleem Trice, Robin Raines, Jacinta Raines, Jada Raines, Janea Raines, Gus Dismukes Jr., Dolly Henry, Angelique Miller, Martha Robinson, Rashidah Robinson, Kit F. Robinson, Latima Jeter, Tracy Smith, Raquel Smith, Richard Domio, Evelyn Green, Alexis McGuinness, Darren Thompson, Ryan Thompson, Alice Walter, Spenser Flag, Ashley Coppola, Lillian Scott, Bob Ryan, Donna Ryan, Hank Testa, Jimmy Thomas, Curtis Roundtree, Shirley Cummins, Malcolm Cummins, Jonathan Cummins, Bianca Domio, Claire Counihan.

John Thompson
Weehawken, New Jersey

Authors' Note

THINK OF YOURSELF as a time traveler, a visitor who has just gone back to a Virginia plantation in 1859 at Christmastime.

The Big House is awash with light and color. Elegance and beauty dazzle your eyes at every turn. There's plenty of food and warm hospitality. But, the people seem uneasy. Listen to their conversations. They're talking about John Brown's raid on Harpers Ferry, slave insurrections, secession, and possible war!

Now, take a walk to the slave Quarters. There is no grandeur here. The wretchedness is staggering. People live in cramped one-room cabins with dirt floors. Yet, there's a celebration going on — eating, singing, and dancing. Does this mean the slaves are happy and contented? No. Listen carefully to their songs and stories. They are mostly of the hope that freedom is coming soon!

The holiday revelers have no way of knowing that an era is coming to a close. Within five years the slaves will be free and the plantation system destroyed. Their way of life will be changed forever. *Christmas in the Big House, Christmas in the Quarters* is a true account of this last Yuletide celebration before the Southern Rebellion.

The events and customs we describe in the book are historically accurate. The conversations and dialogue are real; so is the setting. However, everything we use could not and would not have happened on one plantation. For this reason, we recreated a "Big House" and "Quarters" based on real people, events, and places located in Virginia, 1859. Why Virginia? Because, the Jamestown Colony is where the first American Christmas was observed, and where many of our present holiday traditions began.

Remember while you're reading that this is more than a seasonal account. It is the story of a region and its people on the eve of a war. When that war ended, the great plantations were never the same.

Patricia and Fredrick McKissack
1994

Christmas Is Coming . . .

THE CROPS have been harvested and sold, and the fields laid by till spring; the days have grown shorter and cooler, and the nights come faster and last longer. Then comes the morning of the first frost.

To the child in the Big House the world appears covered by a lace tablecloth as delicate and fine as the one on Mama's dining table.

To the child in the Quarters the woods and fields are in the season of rest, comfortably sleeping inside a gauzy cocoon, until it is time to wake again come spring thaw.

Each child is reminded of the old tale that says the first frost is really stardust sprinkled over the land by the archangel Gabriel, sent to announce the Coming.

Even those who have outgrown the tale in truth accept it in spirit. For with the coming of the first frost, everybody on the plantation — young and old, slave and master — knows that the "Big Times" can't be far off.

IN THE BIG HOUSE . . .

the youngest child asks impatiently, "How long before Christmas, Papa?"

The father smiles. He shows the boy a calendar, and together they count the days to the 25th of December. Thirty-five days!

"Can't you make Christmas come any sooner, Papa?"

AND IN THE QUARTERS . . .

a small child has been asking since strawberry season, "Ma. When will the Big Times come again?"

"Not long after shoe-wearing time."

"How long will the Big Times last?"

"Massa say as long as the Yule log burns. And we've found a big, water-soaked stump down by the creek that should simmer from Christmas Eve to New Year's. A week of Sundays!"

Getting Ready
for the Big Times

TWO MONTHS BEFORE CHRISTMAS, 1859

RIGHT AFTER the first frost, it's slaughtering time. Massa pulls everybody out of the fields. Slave men do the butchering. Slave women boil the fat to make soap. Then they dress the meat, pack it in salt or sugar or honey, and cure it over smoldering hickory coals. The smokehouse is overflowing with hams, sausage, bacon, turkey, venison, fish, and all kinds of wild game.

Then it's clean-up, fix-up time. All hands are used to help get the grand old mansion ready for the season.

Hear the men singing while they work. Say it makes the burden lighter.

> *Mary had a baby . . . yes she did*
> *Mary had a baby . . . yes she did*
> *Oh, Mary had a baby . . .*
> *Born a long, long time ago*

The huge columns out front are white-washed and a new porch railing is built. The gardens are raked and the barns cleaned out. Tools are repaired and stored away. The plantation blacksmith refits the Missus's carriage and reshoes Massa's prize stallion.

Meanwhile, the Missus gives orders to the women slaves.

Wash the windows inside and out, and scrub every floor from top to bottom. Polish the wood furniture, banisters, and mantels with beeswax.

Hear the women singing while they work. Word tell it makes the time go faster.

> *The baby was a boy . . . yes he was*
> *The baby was a boy . . . yes he was*
> *The baby was a boy . . .*
> *Born a long, long time ago*

The rugs are rolled up, taken outside, and beaten dust-free. Mattresses are turned and new ticking sewn on the pillows. Silver is polished, and the crystal chandeliers are taken apart piece by piece and carefully washed in vinegar-water to make them sunshine-bright.

Two weeks before Christmas the Big House is ready — sparkling clean, fresh-smelling, and polished to a dazzle.

Working on the Big House from sunup till sundown doesn't leave much time for the slaves to see after themselves. But late in the evening, when the day's work is over, and early in the morning, before the work day begins, the slaves make the Quarters ready for the Big Times, too.

Fathers stuff cracks with rags to keep out winter winds, and the stone fireplaces are shored up good 'n' strong. Mothers start smiling, humming all the time. Children start minding their elders, doing their chores without being told, like sweeping the common yard and their own cabin floors.

When it is morning but not yet daylight, an old slave woman goes gathering in the woods. Sometimes the children from the Big House and the Quarters go along. The Old One teaches the children as she moves through the brush, carefully snipping wild herbs and pulling roots. She tells them that Wise Men brought little Jesus three gifts, of gold, sweet-smelling spices, and bitter herbs.

By mid-morning the gatherer brings back late fruits and berries to be pickled, spiced, or dried. The roots and herbs will be used to season food and make medicines. She passes out cedar moss, which makes yellow dye; walnut, which yields a deep brown color. But everybody lines up for a bit of elm, cherry, and

red oak; combined they make red . . . *red,* the favorite color in the Quarters. What could be prettier than a pretty red dress for the Christmas dance?

Most of the time, there's no need for fancy clothes — having to work in the fields day in, day out. But the Big Times don't come but once a year. Nobody wants to look bad or feel bad then. Plenty of time to do that all year. Mothers use leftover material from the Big House to make a shawl, an outfit for baby, or a head wrap to wear to a Christmas wedding.

Parents find other throw-away items from the Big House and create new gifts for a son or daughter, especially one who lives on another plantation: a straw doll, a whistle, a gee-haw stick.

Oh, will you wear red? Oh, will you wear red?
Oh, will you wear red, Milly Biggers?
"I won't wear red,
It's too much lak Missus' head.
I'll wear me a cotton dress,
Dyed wid copperse an' oak-bark."

Oh, will you wear blue? Oh, will you wear blue?
Oh, will you wear blue, Milly Biggers?
"I won't wear blue,
It's too much lak Missus' shoe.
I'll wear me a cotton dress,
Dyed wid copperse an' oak-bark."

Now, will you wear black? Now, will you wear black?
Now, will you wear black, Milly Biggers?
"I mought wear black,
Case it's de color o' my back;
An' it looks lak my cotton dress,
Dyed wid copperse an' oak-bark."

A boy has done extra chores for the Missus to earn a piece of lace for his grandmama. She uses it to turn an ordinary dress into something special. She say, "Got to get all the sewing done before Christmas week though, 'cause clothes sewn at that time never wears well."

Late into the night, a young bride lovingly mends her new husband's torn work shirt. Tomorrow she'll dye plain white material his favorite color, and stitch him up a Sunday-go-to-meeting shirt, and herself a matching skirt.

Several weeks before Christmas the Quarters are buzzing with excitement and anticipation. Everybody's busy. Got to get everything ready before the visiting passes are handed out. It won't be long now. Christmas Day's just 'round the corner.

They named the baby Jesus . . . yes they did
They named the baby Jesus . . . yes they did
They named the baby Jesus . . .
A long, long time ago

That was the first Christmas . . . yes it was
That was the first Christmas . . . yes it was
That was the first Christmas . . .
A long, long time ago

Deck the Halls

Two weeks before Christmas

PUTTING-UP-THE-TREE DAY is almost as exciting as Christmas Day itself. Although some neighbors wait until Christmas Eve to put up their tree, Massa puts his tree up early so his family can enjoy it longer.

Massa and several slaves ride to a neighbor's piney woods. Massa's been welcomed to choose a large fir for his family. The slaves chop it down and drag it back to the Big House, along with other woodland greenery picked up along the way.

Once the tree is inside the house and fixed so it won't fall over, the Missus takes over. The children have been sent to another part of the house. Several generations of women busy themselves arranging holly, evergreen boughs, and fir branches over the doors, around the mantels, mirrors, and pictures. Next, they dress the tree in handmade ornaments: string popcorn, cotton balls, gilded nuts and berries, cookies, paper garlands, colored pieces of glass, and white lace. Next they add burgundy velvet and pink satin ribbons, and an assortment of miniature toys, dolls, and furniture.

They hardly notice a young maid who serves tea and passes out ginger cakes to the ladies who are busily sharing stories from Christmases past. "Remember the year all the boys got pocketknives and used them to pop all the acorns off the mantelpiece? Papa tanned their hides good."

It takes all day, but at last the grandchildren, nieces, nephews, and cousins — all the children who have come to share the

holidays in the Big House — are allowed to come into the large parlor. Wide-eyed little ones, breathless with excitement, sigh when they see the shimmering, shining Christmas tree. Why, it looks good enough to eat.

The grandmother tells them about Charles Minnegerode, the German immigrant, who in 1842 had introduced the Christmas tree to a well-known Virginia family. "I shall never forget spending Christmas Eve at the Tucker House in Williamsburg, where I first saw a decorated tree," she remembers. "That was fifteen years ago, but see how the tradition has spread throughout the South. Even Yankees have Christmas trees in their houses now, since President Franklin Pierce put one in the White House several years ago."

Meanwhile, a visiting aunt teaches the family a new carol from Austria: "Silent Night, Holy Night."

Grandpapa complains loudly about foreigners — especially German immigrants, who he says are in league with trouble-making abolitionists. They spirit away slaves on an Underground Railroad. "Northern meddlers all! What will it take for them to let states take care of their own business — secession?"

An aunt, equal his years, tells him to be quiet. Nobody wants to hear a thing about Virginia seceding from the Union. "How could there be a United States without Virginia? Why, we're the Mother Colony, the first of the Thirteen Colonies."

But the fiery old man rambles on, reminding them about the insurrections led by the slaves Gabriel and Nat Turner. "Have you forgotten what happened on board the *Creole*?" His rantings are respectfully dismissed by everyone, except the servant who is pouring hot cider. She listens carefully to find out just how much old Grandmassa really knows.

The mistress is angry. Christmas isn't the time to be concerned about secession, slave revolts, and the like. "Certainly it won't come to that . . . will it?"

A quick-thinking guest begins another carol. They all join in, drowning out Grandpapa's warnings that unless a president who is for states' rights is elected in 1860, "secession will come!"

Each child is assigned a Bible verse to have memorized for Christmas Day. Mama writes Christmas letters to friends and family in distant places. Meanwhile Papa reads from a book sent to him by a London business associate: *A Christmas Carol,* by Charles Dickens. Soon it is bedtime. Papa promises to finish the story about the miserly Ebenezer Scrooge in the coming evenings. The children take one last glance at the beautiful tree, then scurry off to bed.

On the Saturday before Christmas, the slaves decorate the Quarters. Their children help. There is no money to buy velvet, satin, or lace. Still the slaves make do by using what they find in nature.

Children of all ages eagerly rush toward the woods, searching for greenery, pinecones, gourds, shells, and colorful leaves that their mothers will turn into wonderful decorations for tables, windows, and doors. Happy boys and girls skip and dance; happy voices shout and sing whenever a new treasure is discovered. Then it's back to the Quarters to share their bounty.

Wild sprigs of evergreen are put on each door to ward off evil spirits. It is a superstition learned from Scottish and Irish masters of long ago.

One woman ties a red bow on the greenery to add color; others sew or pin dried flowers on a broom, a bucket, or a pot to make them more appealing.

As they work, the children are taught a song, believed to be the oldest American Christmas carol, sung, no doubt, by colonial slave women.

Oh chullun, Christ is come
To heal you of yo' danger;
Pray that you may be reconciled
To the Child that lays in the manger

Cinnamon-soaked apples are hung from the ceiling on different lengths of string — one for every child in the cabin. The trick is for children to bite a plug out of an apple without using their hands. If they succeed they can have the whole apple! Some don't try to bite the apple, choosing instead to let its scent fill the cabin. The memory of a cinnamon-filled house will last a lifetime, and forever be associated with Christmas.

Night brings a chill. Families gather around fires for warmth, but a storyteller warms their hearts with a hopeful tale. The children love the old tale-spinner; his words are magic. They can chase away a fear or make sad eyes smile. Sometimes he tells jokes, sometimes riddles.

I done run out ter happy Wiggy-waggy (child wiggles fingers)
An' I seed ol' Tom Tiggy-taggy (child wiggles toes)
I holler ter brown Wiggy-waggy (wiggles fingers)
Ter drive Tom Tiggy-taggy (wiggles toes)
Thar he go, happy Wiggy-waggy! (wiggles fingers and toes)

I saw Esau kissin' Kate,
An' the truth is that we all three saw.
For I saw Esau, he saw me,
An' she saw I saw Esau.

Tonight the storyteller stills fidgety children with the story of Baby Moses, who was left amongst the bulrushes way down in Egyptland. He ends his story with a song:

Go down, Moses
Way down in Egyptland
Tell Ol' Pharaoh
To let my people go

The adults hear the story and song and take comfort in knowing that "the love that God showed Israel wasn't all on Israel spent. . . ." A deliverer is coming soon.

Then scoot. Off to bed. The children dream about the joys of Christmas yet to come — enough to eat, a clean shirt, a chance to see a loved one.

Christmas Eve — A Very Busy Day

SATURDAY, DECEMBER 24, 1859

CHRISTMAS EVE belongs to the children in the Big House and also in the Quarters. They're all eager to please and be pleased. No time for sour dispositions and peevish tempers. Happy voices, hands, and feet celebrate each minute from morning till night.

As soon as they are able to saddle a horse, the boys in the Big House begin Christmas Eve with a morning pheasant or blue-winged teal hunt. It is great to be included in the company of their father and grandfather and other members of the Improved Order of the Red Men.

Beginning the hunt at sunrise and riding behind the hounds in the brisk December air lifts the spirits. It makes them hungry, too. That's why the mid-morning Hunter's Brunch is a holiday favorite.

The girls go with their mother, aunts, and cousins on short visits to neighbors' houses to see the sick and shut-in, greet out-of-town guests, and personally pass out invitations to the New Year's Eve ball.

Meanwhile, relatives and friends arrive at the mansion all day. A nephew is home from Virginia Military Institute. How grown-up he looks in his uniform. Friends from Fauquier County, aunts and uncles from Richmond, and cousins from as far away as North

18

Carolina are greeted by house servants who show them to their rooms.

A few guests have brought their personal slaves, who are shown how to heat water for baths and other needs. Visiting slaves sleep on the floor in the hallway, or with friends or family in the Quarters.

An early afternoon nap refreshes everyone for the long evening ahead.

Christmas Eve morning in the Quarters is bustling with anticipation — some slaves leaving and others coming.

At last, the master hands out passes to the slaves he's allowing to spend the holiday week with a family member on a nearby plantation. Shout hallelujah! A husband's gon' get to visit his wife. Clap your hands and jump for joy! A daughter's gon' get to visit her mammy. It's reunion time for families sold away from their loved ones. They'll be together again . . . if only for a little while.

A daughter proudly stands next to a notch in the wall to show how much she's grown since Pappy's last visit. A son picks up his mother and turns her 'round and 'round. She's surprised at how much he's grown in a year's time.

All day, there are shouts of excitement and tears of joy — some slaves leaving and others coming. It is Christmas Eve.

Visitors are welcomed because they bring messages from those who weren't granted passes. Everybody gathers at one cabin to hear the news from Berkley, Chippokes, Shirley, Edgewood, and other Tidewater Plantations along the James River. Who has died? Who has married? given birth? got religion? been sold?

Then, making sure none of Massa's spies are close at hand,

somebody asks the one question that's on all their minds — who has run off . . . and made it to freedom?

A copy of the *North Star* newspaper, published by the runaway slave Frederick Douglass, is smuggled into the Quarters. The secret reader shares Douglass's words about freedom and the abolitionist movement. Say they've raised the reward on po' Harriet's head. Could it be true? Are there really white people who are willing to fight so that slavery might end? What manner of men and women are these — William Lloyd Garrison? Sojourner Truth? Harriet Tubman? Charles Sumner?

Talking about abolitionists inspires a song:

> *Behold that star! Behold that star up yonder*
> *Behold that star! Behold that star up yonder*
> *Behold that star of Bethlehem*

Singing fills the Quarters and spills into the woods as the men begin the Christmas Eve possum hunt.

Gloria in Excelsis Deo

CHRISTMAS EVE NIGHT

NIGHT COMES EARLY in December. But it is not a fearful darkness. The stars bathe the fields and woods in a soft blue light. Friendly laughter floating out of the Big House and down to the Quarters robs the wind of its winter sting. It is Christmas Eve night. According to Shakespeare it is a magical night when:

> *"No fairy takes, nor witch hath power to charm,*
> *So hallow'd and so gracious is the time."*

In the Big House, family and guests gather in the large parlor. The master lights the Yule log. Holding with tradition and ancient superstitions, each person casts sprigs of holly into the fire to rid the house and their lives of evil spirits.

The mistress's oldest sister tells the story of the first Christmas tree.

"On the night the Christ Child was born, all creation greeted Him, even the trees. Each tree had something to offer the Babe: fruit, shade, or its exquisite wood. The fir tree was heartbroken because it had nothing to give."

At this point the guests — the children up front — are led to the porch where another fir tree has been decorated with small candles.

All the slaves from the Quarters have been asked to join the

family. Some come willingly. However, since it is one of the few times they have a choice, some slaves choose not to accept this once-a-year invitation, even though they know the master makes a mental note of who is and isn't present. It may turn out to be costly when Massa passes out favors.

The aunt finishes the story. "The stars felt sorry for the poor fir and came down from the sky to adorn it. The Christ Child saw the lighted tree and blessed it. From that day forward the fir has been green always: evergreen."

The youngest child is lifted, so she can place a gilded star on top. And one by one, the candles are lit.

"Ahhhhh! Lovely . . . elegant . . . just plain pretty . . ."

Another young visitor from New Orleans is invited to sing. His voice rises softly on the night air, adding enchantment to the moment:

> *Angels we have heard on high*
> *Sweetly singing o'er the plains*
> *And the mountains in reply*
> *Echo back their joyous strains*
> *Gloria in excelsis Deo*
> *Gloria in excelsis Deo*

Reverently the families drift back into the house and back to the Quarters — each to finish celebrating this night in separate ways.

Amid giggles and glad shouts, the children in the Big House race upstairs to get their stockings and hang them on the mantel in hopes that Santa Claus will come by and leave gifts of candy, nuts, fruits, and toys. More carols are sung. Then the children are sent off to bed. "Sleep tight," Papa calls to them. "Don't let the bedbugs bite," Mama adds. Tomorrow is another big day.

Amid giggles and glad shouts, the children in the Quarters race back to their cabins to hang their stockings. Grandmama say, "Heard Missus say Massa Andrew Jackson, when he was President of these United States, hung his stockings on the White House mantel back in 1835. Tell me Ol' Santy Claus left him plenty of goodies. Reckon it won't hurt to hang yo' stockings by the fire . . . just to see what'll happen."

Four excited children hang their stockings by the fire, then mind their grandmama's warning that disobedient children get ashes in their stockings instead of goodies. So they go to their husk-filled pallets and wait for sleep. Can they help it if Ol' Man Sleep won't come close their wide eyes?

In the next cabin, children listen to a story told by a visiting slave from New Orleans. Her soft, hypnotic words are a verbal melody.

"Tonight, oh, it be the holiest night of the whole year. Yes. Word tell that on the first Christmas Eve, just 'fore the Little One be borned, say, the animals, they speak. Yes. They speak just like folks, saying many thanks and praises to the Most High. I wouldn't tell you a word of a lie. Listen close, now. They say the critters still speak on Christmas Eve. Carry on conversations in French, English, Spanish, and Cajun. But, don't listen if you chance to come upon a stable full of talkin' animals. No. That's the worst luck ever to fall on yo' poor head. To save yo'self go straightaway and get yo'self a mojo and wear it all year till the next Christmas. And come the next Christmas Eve be particular 'bout passing barns."

A little boy with tired eyes snuggles under his father's arm.

Come to you' pallet now — go to you' res';
Wisht you could allus know ease an' cleah skies;
Wisht you could stay jes' a chile on my bres' —
Little brown baby wif spa'klin' eyes!

Pattin' the Juba

LATE CHRISTMAS EVE NIGHT

THE CHILDREN are asleep in the Big House and in the Quarters, too.

House servants have finished their chores and joined their friends in the Quarters. Now the Big Times can begin. The barn doors are swung open, lanterns are hung, everything is ready for the Christmas Eve barbecue and dance.

Somebody begins to "pat the juba," a favorite dance named after a playful African ghost. Musical instruments are hard to come by, so the slaves have had to make their own. Back during slaughtering time, animal hides were saved and stretched over hollowed-out logs to make drums. Horsehair had been pulled over a gourd to make a stringed instrument.

The clapping or stomping gets louder and merrier as the evening progresses. Grab a partner or just dance by yo'self! Sing:

> *Juba this and Juba that,*
> *Juba killed a yeller cat*
> *Juba this and Juba that,*
> *Hold your partner where you at*

Somebody puts a glass of water on the cook's head and she dances the floor from side to side. Then the young girls take the floor "Cuttin' the Pigeon Wing," flapping their arms and holding their necks stiff.

Here come the courtin' couples, "Going (shaking) to the East

and Going (shaking) to the West," which ends with "kissing the one they love best."

Hours pass. Exhaustion sets in, and one by one the dancers return to their cabins. The day's night is over . . . except for the firekeeper.

He hurries to the Big House, slips from room to room, checking the back logs to make sure they will last all night. Quietly he moves to the big fireplace in the parlor. He smiles. The Yule log glows brightly. It is a good log. Sure to last a "week of Sundays."

> Ole Aunt Kate she bake de cake,
> She bake hit 'hine de garden gate;
> She sif' de meal, she gimmie de dus',
> She bake de bread, she gimmie de crus',
> She eat de meat, she gimmie de skin,
> An' dats de way she tuck me in.

Christmas Gif'

SUNDAY, DECEMBER 25, 1859

OME CHRISTMAS MORNING, folks from the Quarters gather outside the Big House and shout, "Christmas Gif'." Massa comes to the window, and playfully shows disgust at being "caught" in the game of "who can say the greeting first and therefore claim a gift."

Duty dictates that the Master and Mistress of the Big House come down to welcome their first visitors. Missus compliments everyone on the way they look, all dressed in their Sunday best.

Massa invites all the men into his study. For the new field hands, bought since last year, this is the first time they've ever been in the main part of the house.

Massa's study is as big as three cabins. One wall of windows lets the light stream in. Bookshelves line two facing walls, floor to ceiling. An imposing mahogany desk with claw and ball feet is set across from the marble fireplace. Two large fireside chairs look comfortable, but no slave dares take a seat. A young house servant dutifully pokes up the fire, lays on another log, then takes his place with the others.

Massa passes out clothing for the year. (Graciously given and humbly received.) With the wave of his hand, he announces that the smokehouse will be opened, and any cut of meat "my people" want can be taken for the Christmas dinner in the Quarters . . . hams included.

The Missus receives the women and children in the parlor.

They line up, and as their names are called, they come up and get a personal gift.

"Thank you for the handkerchief, Missus."

"Thank you for the earrings."

"Thank you for the pretty red scarf."

Then Missus is given a collective gift of a dozen eggs, perhaps a handmade basket, or a hand-carved candleholder. (Humbly given and graciously received.) It shows she is liked.

There are special treats for the children. They are invited to

help themselves, and they do, a little shy at first. But with a little coaxing, they stuff their stockings to the brim.

Back in the study, Massa has mixed the first batch of his famous eggnog, a recipe passed to him by his father and his father before him. His friend from Tennessee argues that Virginia eggnog is too sweet, too rich, and a perfect waste of good whiskey. Nonsense. What would a Virginia Christmas be without eggnog? It's poured in generous amounts to slave and master. He proposes a toast — long, full of words, and delivered in grandiose style. Everyone takes a sip, followed by applause. Massa refills the cups. He is also filled with the spirit of holiday giving.

From a cabinet, he takes a fiddle and hands it to the slave known as the "music-maker." It is to be used during the holiday dances, but a subtle warning is attached — that the borrowed violin had better be "returned in the same good repair."

After giving each morning visitor another round of eggnog, they join the women in the living room.

Greetings are shared; bows, curtsies, and smiles. A slave elder is asked to say a prayer. It, too, is long and full of words. The children are restless. Amen!

Master and Missus request a song. The slaves sing a carol. Then the children sing one and say Bible verses.

Massa stands as a signal. Good guests know when it's time to go. The house slaves still have chores to do, but the field hands are shown out a side door.

"Thank goodness!" they whisper to each other on the way back to the Quarters. "That is over. The rest of the week is ours!"

Shout! Sing:

> *Go tell it on the mountain,*
> *Over the hills and everywhere;*
> *Go tell it on the mountain*
> *That Jesus Christ is born*

All Day It's Christmas

LATER IN THE DAY

HE CHILDREN in the Big House watch as the slaves hurry back to the Quarters. They want to open their presents and eat treats, too, but Mama says not until after breakfast. It's so hard to be patient, especially when "crackers" are going off in the Quarters. But the children know they must wait!

The cook serves a hearty breakfast of grilled fowl, eggs, ham, fish, hominy grits, and biscuits. The children aren't interested in food. They eat hurriedly. "May we be excused?" Papa nods.

Hooray! Hooray! Christmas is here, at last! To each child's delight the stockings are filled to brimming over with all kinds of toys and candies. The girls squeal with pleasure as they find dolls hidden in the branches of the Christmas tree. There's a horn for brother and a top, wagon, a Jacob's ladder, and blocks, too. Who gets the drum? the pocketknife? Look! There's a small china tea set, and the oldest girl gets a diary.

The adults take joy in watching the children dash from the house shouting, "Merry Christmas! Merry Christmas! Isn't it wonderful? All day it's Christmas!"

It is early morning still, but the hours pass fast. With the children out playing, Missus goes out to the kitchen to supervise the Christmas feast. At first the main cook is insulted by the Missus's presence in the kitchen. "Too many cooks spoil the broth," she grumbles.

But the Missus wants everything just so. "Oh my, the turkey mustn't be overcooked. Gracious me, the pudding can't fall."

The cook decides to let it be. On this day every Missus should be the first cook in her own kitchen. First thing, she prepares the turkey, using her mother's recipe.

ROAST TURKEY

A big eighteen- to twenty-pound turkey
Salt and pepper to taste
One big heaping spoonful of bacon fat
Sage
1 cup chopped celery and onions

Clean turkey inside and out. Rinse in clean water and pat dry. Save the liver, gizzard, and the neck for giblet gravy.

Rub turkey with salt and pepper and sage inside and out. Fill turkey cavity with favorite dressing. If dressing isn't being used, fill the cavity with a cup of chopped celery and onions. Then, rub turkey with bacon fat and cover with a clean white cloth that's been dipped in milk or fat. Roast in a medium hot oven, twenty minutes per pound. Baste often, keeping the cloth moist. Remove the cloth the last half hour, so the turkey skin will brown.

The smell of nutmeg, cinnamon, rosemary, and vanilla float in the air. Although the kitchen is removed from the main part of the house, the Missus worries that lingering food smells will be an embarrassment. She orders a slave to burn eucalyptus leaves to smother the odors.

The menu, set weeks ago, is finally complete. Dozens of fruitcakes have been "ripening" in brandy. Mincemeat pies,

buttermilk pies, pecan pies, jelly layer cakes, and a large variety of tea cakes (cookies) are stored in cabinets called "safes."

When the grandfather clock in the hallway chimes three, supper is served. A bell signals for the dinner procession to begin, led by Massa and his wife. Dressed in formal attire, men and women, walking side by side, file into the dining room. There a delicious feast is served by the house servants:

Mutton, Ham, Venison Steaks
Roast Turkey with Sage Dressing and Gravy
Assorted Vegetables
Fresh Fruit (Pineapple)
Bread Pudding with Sugar Glaze
Desserts
Madeira   Sherry
Coffee

Meanwhile, it's Sunday and Christmas in the Quarters all day. After the Christmas gif' exchange at the Big House, the slaves hold a religious service — just long enough to be respectful, but short enough to hold everybody's attention. There's prayer, testimony, singing, and a closing prayer led by an elder: "Lawd, if dancing is wrong in your sight, then I'm asking that you let the time excuse the sin . . ." Then the women hurry back to their cabins, change into work clothes, and start cooking.

The fireplace is used to cook, heat water, and keep the one-room cabin warm. The slave cook hangs a pot on a crane, and sets it at different heights over the coals to regulate the cooking heat. Most of them don't have but one pot and maybe a skillet. And that pot and skillet "is seasoned and knows how to cook" special dishes like gravied rabbit, smoked ham and red-eye gravy, or mixed greens.

SWEET POTATO PIE
(SLAVE STYLE)

Two big sweet potatoes grown in the garden patch out back

2 cups of sugar (trade with the Big House cook). If not avail-
        able use 1 cup of molasses or honey

¼ pound of butter. Scrape from the insides of the butter churn

2 tsp. vanilla

1 tsp. of cinnamon

½ tsp. nutmeg

If you can't get spices then use a tablespoon of rum

½ cup of milk, if somebody you know gets to milk the cow

4 eggs. Send the children to gather eggs in the hay

Peel cooked sweet potatoes and mash them together with butter, sugar, and spices. Beat eggs and milk together in a separate bowl, then slowly add mixture to the potatoes. Beat mixture briskly until it is creamy and smooth.

Pour potatoes into a pie crust shell. Cook until firm. If you can stick a knife in the middle of the pie and none of the mixture sticks, it is ready. Serve after it has cooled.

In one cabin the pungent smell of red pepper mixed with vinegar delights those who love the spicy flavor of meats prepared this way. Next door, sweet 'taters are roasting in ashes along with a plump, juicy chicken. This is sho' better than leather breeches and fatback.

A mother shows her young helper how to make ashcakes. She teases the shy girl, saying, "Honey, I don't hand my recipes out to just anybody."

First she pours boiling water over cornmeal. The daughter adds a pinch of salt and a bit of molasses. (That's the key

ingredient.) They wrap small amounts in cabbage leaves and place them in the ashes. "Best eatin' ever!"

But it's the preparing of the possum that is taken quite seriously. Children sing outside the window where their mother is working:

De way to cook de 'possum nice
Carve him to the heart
First parbile him, stir him twice,
Carve him to the heart
Den lay sweet tates in de pan,
Carve him to the heart
Nuthin' beats dat in the lan'
Carve him to the heart

At dusk the meal is laid out on a common table for all to share. Every cook brings her own special dish. Christmas in the Quarters is the one time of the year there's enough to eat, and enough time to enjoy a meal with family and friends.

An elder blesses the food and the "hands that prepared it all." He gives thanks for another year's good health, and remembers those who are sick or passed on. Amen! And the feast begins!

Virginny Ham, Roast Chicken, Chitlings, Squirrel
Pickled Pig Feet
Possum and Sweet Potatoes
Poke Salad Greens and Eggs
Cabbage, Squash, and Wild Greens Cooked with Ham Hocks
Ashcakes
Buttermilk, Sassafras Tea,
and Persimmon Wine (homemade)

After dinner in the Big House, the men go into the study, where they can smoke. The women gather in the drawing room, where they are served more desserts. A harpist plays hymns and carols, and a great-aunt sings a solo. Some guests play cards, billiards, or chat while they sip their after-dinner cordials and eggnog.

The children have been served in a separate area away from the adults and are brought in to show off their Christmas clothes, made of fine brocade, velvet, and satin. After reciting Christmas poetry, they pose for a tintype taken by a traveling photographer. Then they are sent off to play again.

Papa stands in front of the big mirror over the fireplace and reads from Charles Dickens' *Sketches by Boz*.

A great-uncle complains that Dickens' writings could stir up trouble, because they contain the seeds of rebellion among the lower classes.

It is Mama's side of the family, so she shushes her father's brother by reminding him that the lower classes wouldn't be reading anyway. So why worry? Papa finishes his reading with:

"Would that Christmas lasted the whole year through (as it ought), and that the prejudices and passions which deform our better nature, were never called into action among those to whom they should ever be strangers!"

Afterwards, he raises his glass in a toast (said to be the favorite of George Washington): "All our friends."

Now, the dancing begins and lasts well into the night.

After the big meal in the Quarters, gifts are presented. Santa visited the children earlier, but slave mothers usually give their children something personal, like an apron, basket, a strip quilt, or a hat. They attach a story or advice to it, so if they are separated by being sold, one from the other, the children will have a memory:

"My mama, your grandmama, made me this apron and told me if I ever had a daughter to pass it on to her. I'm giving it to you now that you're twelve. Keep it clean, like your thoughts and deeds."

Then one of the elders is singled out and given a gift of appreciation from all the neighbors in the Quarters. A hat, a pipe, some tobacco, a carved walking stick draw *oohs* and *aahs* and a few tears.

The music starts and the dancing begins. The folk that don't hold with dancing on Christmas Day, and especially on Sunday, go some distance away to hold religious services or "pit school." Still other slaves choose not to join in. They have freedom on their minds:

> "We eat at Christmas and our bellies scream for food all the rest of the year. Let us not forget Dangerfield Newby and the men who died at Harpers Ferry trying to free us. We should free ourselves!"

Rise Up, Shepherd, an' Foller

LATE CHRISTMAS NIGHT

NOBODY'S REALLY SURPRISED when Massa and Missus and the children visit the Quarters. Everybody knows Massa has come for more than just a social call.

Still the family is made to feel welcome and served whatever is to their liking. Massa loves pickled pig feet, and Missus enjoys ashcake with molasses. The children ask for slices of buttermilk or sweet potato pie.

The dancing and singing continue, but toned down a bit. When Massa is convinced that the slaves are "happy" and their minds are on food and drink and having a good time, then he and his family leave. It is the sullen slave who bears watching, he reminds the overseer.

The high steppin', turning, spinning, reels, rocks, and stomps last way into the night. But at last the fiddle falls silent and the revelers go to their cabins. All but one.

When the house slave puts out the last lights in the Big House, he hears the haunting verse of an old carol, resounding through the lowlands. He pauses to listen. Then moves on:

Foller, foller, rise up, shepherd, an' foller,
Foller the Star of Bethlehem,
Rise up, shepherd, an' foller

If you take good heed to the angel's words,
Rise up, shepherd, an' foller

You'll forget yo' flocks, you'll forget yo' herds,
Rise up, shepherd, an' foller

Foller, foller, rise up, shepherd, an' foller,
Foller the Star of Bethlehem,
Rise up, shepherd, an' foller

The hour is late, but the oldest daughter in the Big House hears the song, too. She is much too excited to sleep. Slipping quietly to the desk, she takes out her diary and writes:

"Surprise was the word used most often on this Christmas Day, and laughter is the sound that made my heart nearly burst from excitement and pure delight. It has been a perfect day, ending with the sweet sound of a happy, contented slave singing a carol. I hope this joy will never end . . . it can't. Pa won't let it."

Meanwhile, a young boy in the Quarters lies on his straw-filled pallet. His little sisters are next to him. They hear the carol, too, and they smile knowingly. It is a signal from their father. He has made connection with a conductor on the Underground Railroad.

"Will Pa make it to freedom?" one sister whispers.

"He's got a good chance. One of the slaves up in the Big House who knows how to write, wrote him a pass. He won't be missed till after the Big Times are over."

"He'll follow the North Star right on up to freedom."

"Will we ever see him again?" the youngest child asks.

"I reckon. Slavery can't last always," the boy tells his sisters. "It can't . . . Pa won't let it!"

Foller, foller, rise up, shepherd, an' foller,
Foller the Star of Bethlehem

We Wear the Mask on New Year's Eve

SATURDAY, DECEMBER 31, 1859

EGGNOGGING VISITS, festivals, horseracing, and balls fill the week between Christmas and New Year's. The largest party is on New Year's Eve — a masquerade ball. Invitations were delivered weeks ago.

Every spare room is filled with family and friends who've come for this grand affair.

Carriages arrive bringing masked guests from Williamsburg and Richmond. Elegantly dressed women in the latest ball gowns are escorted from the riverboat and down a path lined with a double row of slaves, each holding a torch to guide them.

The men gather in the study to smoke and talk politics. One young Marine under Colonel Robert E. Lee's command was at Harpers Ferry when the abolitionist John Brown and his men led a raid. He holds everyone's attention as he describes John Brown's hanging earlier in the month. "His eyes blazed like those of a madman!" A toast is proposed: "God bless Colonel Robert E. Lee for saving Harpers Ferry."

Meanwhile, children lean over the winding staircase to sneak a peak at the guests and try to guess who is who behind the masks. Or what unsuspecting young lady is being lured to a doorway where mistletoe is hung. Who will be bold enough to steal a kiss?

Hiding behind masks, young women flirt, especially with handsome bachelors. The young men play guessing games and

tease one another about what messages the girls might be sending with flower language. "Look at the dark-haired girl standing under the picture of peach blossoms. She's looking right at you, sir. Is she saying, 'My heart is your captive'?"

Dancing brings the men and women together. There's also entertainment, solos, and poetry readings. Musicians and a couple from the Quarters are brought up to the Big House to perform for the guests. Then it's more promenades, Virginia reels, and everybody's favorite — the waltz.

Down in the Quarters, the slaves dance to a different tune. The drivers from other plantations are welcomed because they bring news and provide partners for the cakewalk, a favorite dance on New Year's Eve.

But first the news. A driver who was with his master when John Brown was hanged describes it. "I was there that Friday morning. His eyes were filled with strength and determination. He stopped on his way to the gallows to kiss a black baby. My massa say John Brown was crazy. I say John Brown was Truth marching on. Slavery's comin' to an end . . . and soon!" Amen! Amen!

Somebody starts the music. "Maybe if we sing loud enough they won't hear us crying." And the cakewalk begins.

Dancers move along a square, the boy on the inside, the girl on the outside. Here they come — kicking up their heels, jumping, spinning, turning, and all with such high style and grace. "Clap your hands now. Let the music take over your feet. Look out!"

Oh, but the cakewalk is much more than a dance. It's a contest! The elders, who are too old or too tired to dance, serve as judges. They look at the couples as they pass and judge them on their moves. The winners get a cake.

"Why we do the cakewalk, Granny?"

"Well, it began when we slaves was poking fun at the white folk doing what they call the *minuet*. We put a little of our dancing from the time before, and made us a new dance."

"Why they win a cake, Granny?"

"Boy, now you know how hard it is to come by eggs, butter, sugar, flour, and milk — all at the same time and enough to make a cake! Can't be no better prize than a cake!"

"I'm gon' win that cake next year!"

After the winners cut slices of the cake for themselves, they share the rest of their prize with the other dancers.

First Day

SUNDAY, JANUARY 1, 1860

A T MIDNIGHT the guests in the Big House take off their masks. There are very few surprises.

Guns boom! Crackers blast! The plantation bell rings. Eighteen sixty begins with a bang! Pop . . . Pow . . . Poppoppoppoppop!

There is a sadness in the Quarters. The Big Times are coming to an end. Too soon, the week of Sundays is almost over.

Slave and master pay close attention to traditions and superstitions on New Year's Day. They both believe a bad move can seal your fate for the next twelve months.

In the Big House kitchen, the regular cook takes over. She fixes the first-day-of-the-year feast. Black-eyed peas with ham hocks and sweet potatoes are a must in the Quarters and in the Big House, too. The meal is sure to bring good health and wealth during the coming year. Folk share old sayings and notions all day:

No quarreling on New Year's Day, or you'll be arguing all the rest of the year.

Don't cut that man's hair on New Year's Day. You'll cut his fortune by half.

Chile, don't none of us slaves need no bad luck. So listen close. It's better to do without or give it away than to borrow or lend it on New Year's Day.

Bad luck and sorrow are on the minds of all the slaves. The first day of the year is separation day. Sadness hovers over the slaves like a big smothering hand. The happy holiday songs give way to mournful spirituals. A man sings:

Sometimes I feel like a motherless chile
Sometimes I feel like a motherless chile
Sometimes I feel like a motherless chile
A long, long way from home
A long way from home

About noon, the plantation bell summons all the slaves to the front of the Big House. The master gives each slave a conduct and work report. "You're too lazy. You're too slow. You're a hard worker, a fine example of a good slave."

Then Massa calls the names of those who have been sold or hired out. His voice shows no emotion.

"No sense in screaming, mother. Your daughter is twelve years old — old enough to be the body servant to a fine lady over in Richmond. You'll get to see her next Christmas."

Begging, crying, pleading changes nothing. Massa's decisions are final! He goes back into the Big House. The slaves go back to the Quarters and say their farewells. This is the way it is.

The Big Times are over. Sadness replaces happiness in the Quarters. There is no heart for singing and dancing. Separation is almost too painful to bear. Good-bye! So long. Be seein' you!

How much longer can it go on this way? How long, O Lord? How long?

Come nightfall, the families in the Big House and the Quarters watch as the Christmas tree is taken outside and burned in a

bonfire. (Some neighbors leave theirs up until Epiphany.) The Yule log is put out and given to a slave for safekeeping. It is from the leftover log that next year's log will be started. Even now, there is talk about next year when Christmas comes. . . .

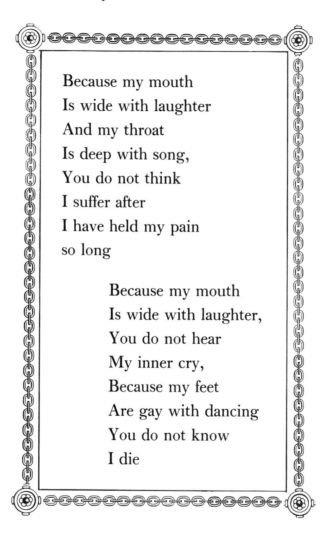

Because my mouth
Is wide with laughter
And my throat
Is deep with song,
You do not think
I suffer after
I have held my pain
so long

Because my mouth
Is wide with laughter,
You do not hear
My inner cry,
Because my feet
Are gay with dancing
You do not know
I die

TO THE BIG HOUSE

"Pa," the Master's daughter whispers. "For Christmas next year, I want my own personal slave. All my cousins have one."

He laughs. "But, you're just ten years old, darling. You don't know the first thing about owning a slave. Maybe when you're

sixteen, all grown-up and a fine lady. Then, you'll know how to be a good mistress."

"That's six whole Christmases from now." The girl counts on her fingers. "December 1865."

"There'll be plenty of slaves for you to choose from then. What about a pretty pony for next year?"

AND TO THE QUARTERS

A slave mother holds her son close. He whispers, "Next year, when the Big Times come, I'm gon' give you a store-bought gift."

The mother smiles. "How so?"

"I'm gon' run away to freedom. . . ."

"Hush," she says, covering his mouth to silence him. "Talk like that will get you in trouble. Besides," she adds, smiling, "the way talk is goin', I got a feeling, we aine gon' need to run away. One day, soon, we gon' celebrate the Big Times in freedom."

Looking Back

THE FAMILIES who celebrated Christmas, 1859, in the Big House and in the Quarters had no way of knowing how much their lives would change in five years. Abraham Lincoln would be elected President in November, 1860, and five days before Christmas, South Carolina would secede from the Union. Edmund Ruffin, Sr., from Virginia would fire the first shot at Fort Sumter on April 12, 1861. On New Year's Day, January 1, 1863, President Lincoln would sign the Emancipation Proclamation, freeing all the slaves in the rebel states, excluding seven counties in eastern Virginia.

Those who ate dinner in the Big House and danced the cakewalk in the Quarters didn't know in 1859 that a war would be fought in their fields and woods. Or that some of the old plantation houses would be burned or used as military headquarters or hospitals. They didn't know that cholera would kill thousands of the newly freed slaves. They didn't know that thousands of soldiers would die, and in the end, General Robert E. Lee would surrender to General Ulysses S. Grant at Appomattox Courthouse in Virginia, April 9, 1865.

The Civil War would end then, and so would the Plantation South, to be remembered in songs and poems, especially at Christmastime when we serve eggnog, put a red bow on our door, sing a carol, or tell a story around the hearth.

NOTES

Page 3

Massa is a slave name for "master." The slaves used *Marse, Marster, Maussa,* and *Mass,* too. Married females were addressed as *Missus,* and *Mis, Little Miss,* or *Missy* if they were young and unmarried.

The large estate with hundreds of slaves is a romanticized view of the antebellum South. Katharine Jones wrote in the introduction to *The Plantation South:* "There was no agreement, even, as to what constituted a plantation, with President Madison insisting that his 3,000 acres at Montpelier was a 'farm' while many a smaller place went by the more pretentious designation of 'plantation.' " Actually, the average slave owner kept one slave woman who served as a cook, housekeeper, and nursemaid, and one slave man who helped in the fields and did other household chores. Sometimes the slave man and woman were married. If they were, their children were sold at about age eight.

In *Before Freedom: When I Just Can Remember*, a collection of slave narratives, Robert Toatley recalled, "My marster was rich. Slaves lived in quarters, three hundred yards from the big house. A street run through the quarters, homes on each side. Beds was homemade. Mattresses made of wheat straw. Bed covers was quilts and counterpanes, all made by slave women."

Most slave cabins were wooden structures about 12' × 12', or 12' × 16', with dirt floors and a crudely cut door. The windows had no panes. As many as ten or twelve people lived in this space where life began and ended.

Pages 7–8

"Gee" is a right turn command given to a horse or mule. "Haw" is the command to turn left. A "gee-haw stick" is an early American, easily made toy. It is made by using two flat pieces of wood about an inch wide and six inches long. Loosely tack them together to form a "t." Make sure the crossbar can spin easily. Hold the toy at the bottom of the "t." When the child yells "Gee," as if by magic, the crossbar will respond by turning to the right. When the child shouts "Haw," the crossbar will swing to the left. Try it. See if it works.

Box: A familiar folk poem from Dudley Randall's *The Black Poets.* Copperse is sulfate of iron.

Page 10

"At Christmas, slaves were generally given a real break from work and often traveled great distances to see families and to celebrate in communal groups.

Blacks and whites, who might share English Christmas puddings and drinks, also celebrated separately but at the same time." (Excerpt from *The World They Made Together*, by Mechal Sobel, p. 67.)

Field slaves got a holiday break from work, but house slaves were expected to continue taking care of their master's needs, e.g. cleaning, heating water for baths, laundry, most of the cooking, and care of the children in addition to their extra holiday duties. Drivers were expected to be on call to take their master and/or his family on short trips and, in some cases, accompany them on long journeys.

Page 11

Slaves listened to household conversations and passed interesting stories and information to those in the Quarters.

Red and green were not associated with Christmas during the Victorian period. Red was considered a vulgar and cheap color. Dyes made from berries were not long-lasting, nor were the colors brilliant. The colors usually faded after one or two washings.

The members of the Carter family, owners of the Shirley Plantation in Virginia, shared a story about a young relative who received a pocketknife for Christmas. He used it to pop all the decorative acorns off the mantelpiece in the large parlor. Many years later, another relative received a pocketknife for Christmas. He proceeded to pop all the rest of the acorns off, too.

Page 13

The Puritans didn't believe in celebrating Christmas with feasting and decorating. There was a law against it. Those caught celebrating Christmas were fined and sometimes beaten. It wasn't until President Franklin Pierce from New Hampshire (1852–1856) celebrated Christmas in the White House that Christmas became a "national" event.

In 1859, "Silent Night" was still considered a new Christmas carol. It was written in 1818 by Joseph Mohr, a young assistant pastor at a church in Oberndorf, Austria. It was set to music by Franz Gruber, the church organist.

Gabriel Prosser led a revolt of 1,000 slaves and several whites in Richmond, Virginia, in 1800. By 1859, Gabriel had become a legendary folk hero. Some slaves refused to believe Gabriel had really been hanged. They sang about "The Escape of Gabriel Prosser" with the help of a friend named Billy.

> *Dere wuz two a-guardin' Gabriel's cell*
> *An' ten more guards in the jail about;*
> *An' two a-standin' at the hangman's tree,*
> *But Billy wuz dere to git Gabriel out.*

Nat Turner led a slave revolt in Southampton County, Virginia, 1831. Thirty whites were killed before he was captured on October 30. Twelve days later, he was hanged.

In 1841, the captives aboard the *Creole* attacked and overpowered the crew. The slaves sailed to the Bahamas where they were granted freedom.

Page 14

Christmas cards weren't in regular use in 1859. People wrote letters and visited instead.

The actual title of Charles Dickens' story is *A Christmas Carol in Prose*, published in London, England, 1843. It became a great success in the United States. Americans received copies from their English friends in time for Christmas readings.

Page 15

Box: This riddle was a favorite of slave children. Wiggy-waggy is a dog who's been sent to get Tom Tiggy-taggy the hog out of the field.

Plantation children enjoyed tongue twisters, which were very popular in the 1850s.

Page 18

The Improved Order of the Red Men was started in Virginia around 1834. It is believed to be one of the oldest secret societies of American origin.

Pages 19–21

Slave owners gave special privileges to slaves who spied for them, bringing information about happenings in the Quarters.

Frederick Douglass, born a slave in Tuckahoe, Maryland, around 1817(?), was, by 1859, a leading abolitionist. When he was a boy, his mistress had taught him how to read. Later, he escaped to New York. There he published his autobiography and a weekly newspaper, the *North Star*.

Drivers had more freedom of movement than either field or house slaves. So they passed messages from one plantation to another, and they often smuggled newspapers and information about the abolitionist movement, too.

The education of slaves was against the law in most Southern states in 1859. But slaves learned to read any way they could. It wasn't unusual for one or more slaves to be "secret readers."

William Lloyd Garrison was a leading abolitionist in 1859. So was Charles Sumner, Senator from Massachusetts. Sumner returned to his duties on December 5, 1859, after recovering from a beating. Preston Brooks, Representative from South Carolina, had gotten so angry with Sumner's anti-slavery position, Brooks had attacked and beaten the Senator with a cane.

Sojourner Truth and Harriet Tubman were former slaves who were also abolitionists.

Page 24

Those who spent the holidays in other parts of the country shared their traditions with family and friends. The child who sang "Gloria in Excelsis Deo," and the slave who told the story about the talking animals (p. 26) were from New Orleans where Christmas celebrations in the 1850s were a unique blend of English, French Catholic, Afro-Caribbean, and Native American cultures.

The "good night" salutation was used during this period. "Sleep tight" was a wish for a comfortable sleep. It referred to rope slats that held the mattress in place. If the bed ropes weren't pulled tightly, the mattress sagged and the bed was uncomfortable. Even in the best of homes, bedbugs — small red mites — were a problem. They often infested mattresses and bed covers and made it impossible for a person to get a good night's sleep. "Don't let the bedbugs bite" was an added wish for comfort.

Candle-lighted Christmas trees were a fire hazard. Some plantation houses put lighted trees on or near a porch. Slaves were not allowed to have lighted trees. A stray spark could wipe out the shanties in the Quarters.

Page 26

The poem is the last stanza of Paul Laurence Dunbar's "Little Brown Baby." Although Dunbar (1872–1906) wrote long after slavery had ended, his mother told stories about plantation life. Dunbar used her language patterns and stories in his poetry.

Page 27

Instrument-making was a skill Africans brought to the Americas. The banjo is of African origin. Since many Africans could communicate with drums, some states passed laws forbidding slaves to make drums.

Page 29

Box: This folk song "Ole Aunt Kate" was one of many songs and stories about fictional slave women named Aunt Kate, Aunt Dinah, and Aunt Dicey.

Page 34

Slave children made crackers (similiar to our modern-day firecrackers or balloons) from hog bladders, saved from slaughtering time. The children blew up the bladders like balloons, then popped them. All plantation children — whites and blacks — enjoyed popping "crackers."

A Jacob's ladder is a string puzzle, but it was also one of the earliest mechanical toys made in the United States. One model made in Virginia was a ladder with a monkey attached to it. When the ladder was turned, the monkey turned and flipped up and down the ladder.

Page 35
Box: This nineteenth-century recipe for roast turkey seems to have originated in Virginia, spreading into more southern states before it was adopted by northerners.

Page 37
During the colonial period, pineapples had to be imported so they were rare and very expensive. Hosts who served their guests pineapple were considered generous and gracious. By 1859, pineapples had become a symbol of hospitality, so it was a common motif used in architecture, furniture, and other decorative pieces. A number of Virginia plantations use the pineapple in their architectural design, especially those located in the Tidewater area.

Page 38
Box: The sweet potato pie recipe is based on information from slave narratives and plantation diaries.

Pages 40–41
Slaves didn't have big feasts often. Their everyday meals were far less elaborate. Slave narrators often talked about the biting hunger that hounded them daily. Frederick Douglass, who had been a slave, wrote in his autobiography that Christmas was the one time slaves got enough to eat and enough time to eat it.

It was considered socially rude for nineteenth-century women to stay in the same room while men were smoking, drinking "hard" liquor, and/or talking politics, so the women gathered in the "drawing room," which is short for "withdrawing room."

In 1839 photography was introduced to the world by Frenchman Louis Jacques Mande Daguerre. Daguerreotypists were popular until about 1851, when an Englishman, Frederick Scott Archer, originated the *collodion* process of making negatives. Glass was used first, followed by tin, which was inexpensive and more portable. In the late 1850s the traveling tintype photographers were commonplace.

Page 43
In 1859 the exchange of gifts among adults wasn't common practice. Christmas gifts were for children and slaves. However, the slaves valued gifts given by loved ones; they never knew when they might be separated.

A strip quilt is a design made by African-American slaves, but can be traced to the West Coast of Africa. Swatches of cloth are sewn together to a desired length. The long, narrow strips are sewn together to form a quilt.

Page 44

Some slaves refused to celebrate Christmas. They used the time off to study or plan an escape. Some defiant slaves held "pit schools" out in the woods. They dug a deep pit in the ground large enough for two or three people to sit in. Then they threw covers over the hole to hide the light they used to read and study.

Dangerfield Newby was a forty-four-year-old free black man whose wife and seven children were still slaves. He had offered to buy his wife's and children's freedom, but each time, their master raised the price. Newby's wife wrote him, "Oh Dear Dangerfield, come this fall without fail, money or no money. I want to see you so much." Newby joined John Brown hoping to free his family, but Newby was the first to be killed during the raid.

John Brown, 59, and 18 followers (13 whites and 5 blacks) attacked Harpers Ferry in Virginia. The 5 African Americans at Harpers Ferry were: Lewis Sheridan Leary, Dangerfield Newby, John Anthony Copeland, Shields Green, and Osborn Perry Anderson. Leary and Newby were killed; Copeland and Green were captured and hanged; and Anderson escaped. Brown was captured and hanged on December 2, 1859. While still in jail, he wrote a note which said in part:

> "I, John Brown, am now quite certain that the crimes of this guilty land will never be purged away but with blood . . . "

Page 54

Masters sometimes "hired out" slaves to work on neighbors' farms. The slave did the work, but the master was paid.

Adelene Jackson recalled in *Before Freedom: When I Just Can Remember*, "Marster never sold a slave, but swaps were made with kinpeople to their advantage."

Page 56

Box: Although Langston Hughes was a twentieth-century poet, this poem reflects the feelings of most slaves on the eve of the Civil War, 1859.

BIBLIOGRAPHY

Andrews, Wayne. *Pride of the South — A Social History of Southern Architecture*. New York: Atheneum Publishing Company, 1979.

Bennett, Lerone, Jr. *Before the Mayflower — A History of Black America*. Chicago: Johnson Publishing Company, Inc., 1987.

Blassingame, John W. *The Slave Community — Plantation Life in the Antebellum South*. New York/Oxford: Oxford University Press, 1979.

Bontemps, Arna. *American Negro Poetry*. New York: Hill and Wang Publishing Company, 1963.

Comstock, Helen. *American Furniture*. New York: Viking Press, 1962.

Culff, Robert. *The World of Toys*. New York: Paul Hamlyn Publishing Company, 1969.

Dance, Daryl Cumber. *Shuckin' and Jivin': Folklore from Contemporary Black Americans*. Bloomington: Indiana University Press, 1978.

Dunbar, Paul Laurence. *Lyrics of a Lowly Life*. New York: The Citadel Press Book, published by Carol Communications, 1984 edition.

Fox-Genovese, Elizabeth. *Within the Plantation Household — Black and White Women of the Old South*. Chapel Hill: University of North Carolina Press, 1988.

Gates, Henry Lewis, Jr. *The Classic Slave Narratives*. New York: The New American Library, 1987.

Genovese, Eugene D. *Roll Jordan Roll: The World the Slaves Made*. New York: Vintage Books — A Division of Random House, 1974.

Gross, Linda, and Marian E. Barnes, eds. *Talk That Talk: An Anthology of African-American Storytelling*. New York: Simon and Schuster Publishers, 1989.

Grow, Lawrence. *The Fifth Old House Catalogue*. Pittstown: The Main Street Press, 1986.

Hurmence, Belinda, ed. *Before Freedom: When I Just Can Remember*. Winston-Salem: John F. Blair Publishers, 1990.

Jones, Katharine M. *The Plantation South*. Indianapolis and New York: The Bobbs-Merrill Company, Inc., 1957.

Kane, Harnett T. *The Southern Christmas Book*. New York: David McKay Company, Inc., 1958.

Kimball, Marie. *Thomas Jefferson's Cook Book*. Richmond: Garrett and Massie Incorporated, 1949.

Lane, Mills. *Architecture of the Old South*. Savannah: The Beehive Press, 1987.

Langstaff, John. *What a Morning! The Christmas Story in Black Spirituals.* Illustrated by Ashley Bryan. New York: Margaret McElderry Books, 1987.

Lewis, Jan. *The Pursuit of Happiness — Family Values in Jefferson's Virginia.* Cambridge: Cambridge University Press, 1983.

Morgan, Edmund S. *American Slavery/American Freedom.* New York: W.W. Norton and Company, Inc., 1975.

O'Neal, William. *Architecture of Virginia.* New York: Virginia Museum/Walker and Company, 1968.

Randall, Dudley. *The Black Poets.* New York: Bantam Books, 1971.

Rollins, Charlemae. *Christmas Gif'.* Chicago: Follett Publishing Company, 1963.

Rothery, Agnes. *Houses Virginians Have Loved.* New York: Bonanza Books, a division of Crown Publishing Company, 1953.

Simon, Henry. *Christmas Songs and Carols.* Boston: Houghton Mifflin Company, 1955.

Spaulding, Henry D., ed. *Encyclopedia of Black Folklore and Humor.* Middle Village: Jonathan David Publishers, 1990.

Walklet, John J. Jr. *A Window on Williamsburg.* Photographs by Taylor Biggs Lewis, Jr. New York: Holt, Rinehart and Winston, 1966.

Wiley, Bell Irvin. *Confederate Women.* Westport: Greenwood Press, 1975.